Looking at . . . Stegosaurus

A Dinosaur from the JURASSIC Period

Weekly Reader®
BOOKS

Published by arrangement with Gareth Stevens, Inc.
Newfield Publications is a federally registered trademark
of Newfield Publications, Inc. Weekly Reader is a federally
registered trademark of Weekly Reader Corporation.

Library of Congress Cataloging-in-Publication Data

Amery, Heather.
  Looking at-- Stegosaurus/written by Heather Amery; illustrated by Tony Gibbons.
      p. cm. -- (The New dinosaur collection)
  Includes index.
  Summary: Describes the physical characteristics and probable behavior of this peaceful giant
of the Jurassic.
  ISBN 0-8368-1047-3
  1. Stegosaurus--Juvenile literature. [1. Stegosaurus. 2. Dinosaurs.] I. Gibbons, Tony, ill.
  II. Title. III. Series.
  QE862.O65A45 1993
  567.9'7--dc20   93-5535

This North American edition first published in 1993 by
Gareth Stevens Publishing
1555 North RiverCenter Drive, Suite 201
Milwaukee, Wisconsin 53212 USA

This U.S. edition © 1993 by Gareth Stevens, Inc. Created with original © 1993 by
Quartz Editorial Services, Premier House, 112 Station Road, Edgware HA8 7AQ U.K.

Consultant: Dr. David Norman, Director of the Sedgwick Museum of Geology,
University of Cambridge, England.

Printed in the United States of America

Weekly Reader Books Presents

Looking at . . . Stegosaurus
A Dinosaur from the JURASSIC Period

by Heather Amery
Illustrated by Tony Gibbons

THE NEW
DINOSAUR
COLLECTION

Gareth Stevens Publishing
MILWAUKEE

Contents

Introducing
Stegosaurus

Stegosaurus (STEG-OH-SAW-RUS) was a large and strange-looking dinosaur whose bones have been found in North America. It may have seemed fierce but was really very peaceful. However, it could put up a good fight if attacked by one of the giant, meat-eating dinosaurs who thought it would make a good meal.

The double row of plates along its back, ending in a spiked tail, puzzled scientists for a long time. What were they for? Were they perhaps used to protect **Stegosaurus** from the teeth and claws of other dinosaurs? Or did **Stegosaurus** use the plates to cool down or warm up its body?

Could it move them and even lay them down flat? Or were they just for decoration?

And, scientists have asked, since **Stegosaurus** had such a small brain, was it the least intelligent dinosaur of all?

You will find the answers to many questions about **Stegosaurus** on the following pages.

Spot one!

Stegosaurus is easy to recognize because of the rows of plates that stick up all the way along its body.

It was a big dinosaur, about as long as two large cars. You would probably only have come up to its knees.

Its back legs were about twice as long as its front legs, and it plodded along slowly with its head fairly close to the ground.

The other very noticeable thing about **Stegosaurus** was its tail. It was a powerful, thick tail – with long spikes – that tapered toward the end. **Stegosaurus** swished it from side to side as it moved.

Each spike of **Stegosaurus's** tail was about 3 feet (1 m) in length. The spikes were made of bone and were very sharp, making useful weapons for self-defense when an enemy approached. **Stegosaurus** often had to protect itself against fierce predators that wanted to eat it.

Stegosaurus had a small, narrow head that was tiny compared with its body. Its mouth had a beak. Since it was a herbivore, eating only vegetation, it used its beak to tear off all the soft plants, leaves, and ferns that it ate. **Stegosaurus** chewed these with the rows of small, weak teeth that were at the back of its jaw. It probably stored food for several days in its large stomach.

7

Magnificent skeleton

From its remains, we know **Stegosaurus** had very strong bones to hold up the weight of its heavy body. But the most surprising thing about its structure are the two rows of large, flat plates that stood upright on its neck, all the way along its back, and then right down its tail.

These plates were smaller near its head and toward the tail. The largest plates were in the middle of its back.

The bony plates were not fixed to the main skeleton. At the end of the tail were four sharp spikes **Stegosaurus** used for self-defense.

When **Stegosaurus** was first discovered, scientists were puzzled by something about its skeleton.

Later, however, other scientists decided that the hole held lumps of a chemical called glycogen. Some animals and birds alive today also have glands that release this chemical. It supplies their muscles with extra energy when they need to fight or run away from danger.

What was the space in its backbone near the hips? Some thought **Stegosaurus** might have had another brain there to control its huge body. (Its head, as you can see, was tiny in comparison with the rest of its body, and the brain in its head was the smallest of all the dinosaurs that have been discovered so far.)

Stegosaurus had stumpy feet like an elephant. It plodded along on all fours but could also stand on its back legs to feed from trees. Its legs were designed to support its weight, not for speedy running. So, if a hungry carnivore approached, **Stegosaurus** would not have had much success in escaping. It would have had to fight for its life.

When Stegosaurus

Stegosaurus lived in the part of the world we now call North America about 140 million years ago. At that time, in the Jurassic Period, the climate was hot all year round, and it often rained.

There were many other types of dinosaurs roaming the landscape then. Some, such as **Dryosaurus** (DRY-OH-SAW-RUS), below, were a lot smaller. But it was a fast runner and could make a speedy escape.

walked the Earth

The **Kentrosaurus** (<u>KEN</u>-TRO-<u>SAW</u>-RUS), at the bottom right-hand corner of this page, was a smaller cousin of **Stegosaurus.** The dinosaur in the water is a giant, long-necked **Brachiosaurus** (<u>BRAK</u>-EE-OH-<u>SAW</u>-RUS).

Meat-eating dinosaurs hid in the thickets, waiting to take other dinosaurs by surprise.

Bone Wars

The bones of **Stegosaurus** were first discovered by workers helping a famous American scientist named Othniel C. Marsh. That was about 120 years ago. He had sent teams of men to search for dinosaurs in the wild, rugged country in Colorado and Wyoming, in the United States. They spent years hacking skeletons out of solid rock. It was hard, dangerous work.

At the same time, another famous American scientist – Edward D. Cope – sent fossil hunters to the same parts of the country.

The two men were rivals, both racing to be the first to find and name new dinosaurs.

The two teams often worked only a few miles (km) apart. Sometimes, they even fought over the dinosaur remains they discovered. The rivalry between Marsh and Cope became known as the "Bone Wars."

Both scientists were very successful. Before they started their great search, only nine types of dinosaurs were known to have lived in North America. But between them, these men found 136 different ones. These included the long-necked **Diplodocus** (DIP-LOD-OH-KUS) and fierce **Allosaurus** (AL-OH-SAW-RUS).

Marsh once even found that Cope had put the head on the wrong end of a dinosaur skeleton when reconstructing it! Cope was very embarrassed by his mistake.

Plated dinosaur

Stegosaurus's bony plates are a puzzle. When scientists discovered the first skeletons, they did not know if the plates lay flat on **Stegosaurus's** back or stood upright in rows. If the plates had stuck out sideways, they might have defended **Stegosaurus** against attack.

In fact, **Stegosaurus** got its name – meaning "roof lizard" – because some scientists thought the plates lay flat like the tiles on a roof. But, today, most scientists believe the plates stood up in pairs.

The plates formed a double row right along **Stegosaurus's** back but were not directly opposite each other.

What, then, were the plates for? Some scientists suggest **Stegosaurus** used the plates to control its body temperature so that it was never uncomfortably hot nor too cold.

In the cool mornings, **Stegosaurus** may have held its plates to the Sun for warmth. Perhaps the plates worked like solar panels. But, in the heat of the day, it might have turned the plates sideways, using the breeze to cool down.

Blood vessels ran through these plates. They worked like the pipes in a central heating system. No one is sure, however, why some types of dinosaurs needed these radiators but others did not.

There may also have been another use for the plates. Some scientists think the plates of a male **Stegosaurus** were a very bright color.

The plates of a female may have been smaller and less colorful.

Stegosaurus may have used the plates to attract females during the mating season.

The magnificent plates were smallest at the neck and tail end. They ended on the tail. Behind them were two pairs of bony spikes used for self-defense against predators.

Life in the herd

Stegosaurus probably lived in family herds, with the older members looking after the young ones and guarding them from meat-eaters.

The herds roamed together, looking for fresh plants and leaves to

eat once they had cleared one feeding ground of its vegetation.

The animals had to be on constant lookout for hungry carnivores that might attack at any time.

But what if a **Stegosaurus** was attacked by a meat-eater?

16

Then, the whole herd would come to the rescue, rushing to help it in its hour of need. They would strike the predator with their tails and wound it with the sharp spikes.

After two males challenged each other, they may have charged, lashing their tails and swaying their necks from side to side, crashing shoulder to shoulder and slipping around on muddy ground.

The winner then displayed its brightly

It may have taken three of them to ward off an enemy successfully.

At the start of the mating season each year, the males may have fought each other for the females.

colored plates to the females in order to attract them while the loser plodded away.

Putting up a fight

Stegosaurus plodded quietly along, grazing on ferns. Suddenly, there was a terrifying roar. An **Allosaurus** crashed out of the trees and went straight for **Stegosaurus**, snapping its huge jaws. It was hungry, and **Stegosaurus** looked appetizing.

Allosaurus was a fearsome predator, much bigger than **Stegosaurus.** It had a massive head and huge jaws with many sharp teeth.

Stegosaurus had wandered off from the rest of the herd, so there were no others to protect it against this predator.

Who would strike first? **Allosaurus** gave another threatening roar and leaped at **Stegosaurus.**

18

Stegosaurus would not give up without a fight, however. It lashed its tail at **Allosaurus's** stomach, the spikes gashing the predator's scaly skin.

Allosaurus clawed back viciously. **Stegosaurus** lashed its spiked tail again, giving **Allosaurus's** leg a stunning blow. Both creatures roared angrily.

Allosaurus staggered but managed to close its jaws on **Stegosaurus's** back. Sadly, **Stegosaurus** was no match for this ferocious carnivore.

Stegosaurus data

Stegosaurus was a very large, four-footed, plant-eating dinosaur. It had a long body, a tiny head, a thick tail, and two rows of plates along its neck and back. It plodded along slowly on clumsy feet, its heavy, spiked tail held out behind it.

Tiny brain

Stegosaurus had a brain that was the smallest – compared with the size of its body – of any animal that has ever lived. It was only about as big as a walnut. With such a tiny brain, Stegosaurus could not have been very smart, but it was probably clever enough for its needs.

Small head

Stegosaurus had a very small head for the size of its body. The head was only about as big as a large dog's. It also had a toothless beak that it used for chopping off the leaves on which it fed. Its nostrils were on the top of its head.

Cheek teeth

At the sides of Stegosaurus's jaws were small, weak cheek teeth. It probably did not chew at its meals. Instead, it swallowed stones, which it then used for grinding food in its stomach.

Lashing tail

Stegosaurus's tail was thick and strong. Near the tip of the tail were four bony spikes. These were like built-in weapons. Any predator would have felt their sharp lash. **Stegosaurus** could also prop itself up on its tail when it stood on its back legs to feed from tall trees.

Clumsy feet

Stegosaurus had five toes on each of its front feet and four toes on each of its back feet. The claws on its toes were like small hooves. These hooves were no good for fighting but may have been useful for getting a grip on wet or muddy ground as **Stegosaurus** lumbered along through the Jurassic landscape.

Bony plates

The largest plate on **Stegosaurus's** back was about three times the size of this page. The plates were made of bone with lots of blood vessels around them. The plates were covered with horn or tough, scaly skin. Many scientists agree that they were probably used to control **Stegosaurus's** body temperature.

The Stegosaurid family

Stegosaurus was one of a family, or group, of dinosaurs called **Stegosaurids**. This name means "roof lizards." All members of this family had large, bony plates or spikes all the way along their backs.

Stegosaurus (1) was the largest member of this family and had the biggest plates. It lived in what we now call North America about 140 million years ago.

Kentrosaurus (2) was a similar **Stegosaurid** – but only about half as long as **Stegosaurus**. Its name means "pointed lizard," and it had plates on its neck, too. There were spikes on its back and tail and on its hips. These were used to frighten off larger predators. It also lived about 140 million years ago, and skeletons have been found in Tanzania, Africa.

3

4

Tuojiangosaurus (TOH-<u>WANG</u>-OH-<u>SAW</u>-RUS) **(3)** was a big cousin. Its name means "Tuojiang lizard," and it lived in what is now Zhucheng County, in southern China. It had a double row of 15 plates along its neck and back and four tail spikes. The plates on its back were more cone-shaped than **Stegosaurus's** plates. It carried its head not far from the ground, ready for grazing on plants.

Dacentrurus (<u>DA</u>-SEN-<u>TROO</u>-RUS) **(4)** was a much smaller member of the same family. Its name means "pointed tail." Scientists still do not know a great deal about this dinosaur. But from looking at its remains, they think it probably had a double row of spikes on its back and tail, instead of plates. This **Stegosaurid** lived in what is now western Europe in the Jurassic Period about 160-140 million years ago.

GLOSSARY

carnivores — meat-eating animals.

ferocious — cruel or savage.

herbivores — plant-eating animals.

herd — a group of animals that travels and lives together.

mate — to join together (animals) to produce young.

plates — thin layers or scales of bone or hornlike tissue.

predators — animals that kill other animals for food.

spikes — long, thin, pointed objects usually used to pierce or cut.

thicket — a dense growth of shrubs or small trees.

INDEX